Deliberately
Thirsty

editor
Sean Bradley

Argyll
publishing

This issue is dedicated
to the memory of
Davy White (1923 – 1998)

First published 1998
Argyll Publishing
Glendaruel
Argyll PA22 3AE
Scotland

The authors have asserted their
moral rights.

**British Library Cataloguing-in-
Publication Data.**

**A catalogue record for this book
is available from the British
Library.**

ISBN 1 874640 59 9

Cover
'Exhibition' by Alastair Chisholm

Graphic Manipulator
Graham McQuarrie

Printing
Rowland Digital Printing, Bury St
Edmunds

Thanks to the Bow Bar,
West Bow, Edinburgh
for financial support for this issue

CONTENTS

R. ERIC SWANEPOEL 5
Heart bypass, squid survey
DES DILLON 8
Someone Else's Tune
Siesta
The Rosary Bell
B MacKENZIE GARDINER 10
Jenners Tea
TODD McEWEN 14
With Billy Collins in the Berg Room
SIMON CRUMP 15
Lady in Red
August 1970
Stairway To Heaven
BRIAN McCABE 22
spider
viceroy
OWEN O'NEILL 24
Shoulder Bit
It Was Only Eleven O Clock
IAN MACPHERSON 27
From the Journals of Fiachra MacFiach (vol xxiv)
My Fundamental Friend:
DUNCAN MACKAY 37
Bravehert
Blootert
IAN RANKIN 43
Acid Test
EDDIE GIBBONS 51
Bloke
Icks
LUCY ELLMANN 53
Apple Pie & Barbecue
DAVID TOMASSINI 57
Fragments for a Venetian Epic
A Maitter o' Scale
DILYS ROSE 60
Flesh and Blood
A Hideous Jig

FOREWORD

At Half past Three, a single Bird
Unto a silent Sky . . .

Putting this magazine together required working into the night. At one point the youngest in the family tugged my sleeve helplessly and said, 'Father, this performance poetry, it simply doesn't work on the page'. I patted him on the head and said, 'Don't give up my child – just keep editing'.

At Half past Four, Experiment
Had subjugated test . . .

As the children returned to their keyboards and I poured myself another modest measure of Tullamore Dew, I reassured myself that editors had to start somewhere, and surely this was a sound basis for eradicating pomposity from the profession. Time will tell.

At Half past Seven, Element
Nor Implement, be seen –

But that is for the reader to decide. My hope for *Deliberately Thirsty* is that it moves readers to laugher, to tears but, most of all, to subscribe.

Sean Bradley
Editor
November 1998

R. ERIC SWANEPOEL

Heart bypass, squid survey

The first time you do it it's a weird sensation, right enough, cutting into still-living flesh. Then, like everything, it becomes routine: the blade seems to know where it's going. But it's never just a job. They're all individuals pulsing away, glistening, wet sleeknesses of desperate life trying to communicate for the last time: colour patterns blooming and fading, a jet of ink here, a squirt of water there. Rage, rage against the dying of the light... To call them molluscs seems demeaning. As a scientist you are supposed to be cool and detached, but how can you when you are cutting up something so beautiful and so frantic. The tasks on the ship are banal: weighing, dissecting, measuring and putting aside the now inert little lumps of tissue. You know you will never sound the depths of the secrets of their ephemeral grace in this way, but you tell yourself that it is all for the greater good – for theirs and yours, and mankind's. After all, if we know how many there are, how often they breed, and how fast they grow, then we can exploit them in perpetuity. Nets and stomachs will be filled, fishermen will have jobs, and squid will still be there, colour-throbbing their enigmatic way through the oceans, super-charged pelagic chameleon krakens forever.

The least honour you can do them is to shun their touch. Plunge your hands into their squirminess and connect with the dying spirit of the deep. It's practical too – a firm non-shrinking grip makes for fast and sure work. You have to do it, so do it quickly and well, and get as much as you can from the pillage.

We rise to hear the winch engines hauling the nets in, Janet and I, The British Contingent. On the stern deck we inspect the hoard of wriggling silver strained from the briny. The crew sorts it for us: whiptail hake in one box, common hake in another, then there's kingclip. The boxes in which we're interested are packed with Illex. They're heavy, but not that heavy, and we are young and strong, and so we help Juan to place them on the scales – after all he's over fifty and he's just had a bypass operation. He doesn't thank us, but that's just his way, I suppose. We pull our weight and don't stand on ceremony, which is more than can be said for some...

There they appear now, the Argentinian scientists, late but 'glamorous', plastic chic and waif thin, with all that make-up plastered on their faces, but nothing in their stomachs and less in their hearts – and who could possibly divine what's in their heads? Look at them waiting, obscene caricatures of femininity, waiting for poor Juan to heave their boxes on to the scales, while they affectedly (they must think elegantly) smoke their constant cigarettes. If they ate a bit more and posed a bit less they would be of more use. Why the hell did they bother coming, with their lacquered nails and long blond hair? Their pathetic fingertip poking doesn't get the work done – heaven's sake, if they don't like the sensation of handling squid they could wear gloves! God, their hair-flicking makes me sick.

The Argentinians.

It wasn't our fault that our government invaded the Malvinas. Of course we would lose. Might is right and the English have might, and such interests in our fishing grounds and in our oil of the future – and Thatcher needed the war to stay in power. Thatcher: they're all like her aren't they? Hard men-women bereft of femininity. What are we on earth for, after all? We were so stupid to think that we could win against that ugliness. Yes, we were bound to lose! And now they are on our ship, and glaring at us, those sexless eat-and-work machines, who don't give a damn about aesthetics. It's such a lack of respect for themselves, and for men. We're only in this life so long and the least we can do is appreciate its pleasures – and give pleasure to others. It's not as if men and women are the same! God made us that way, so why do they strain to minimise the difference? It's sick! And once again these blunt Anglo-Saxons are taking our resources from us. One population of squid, they say, not four, so that we can't fish the year round...

Juan.

They cut me open I would have died otherwise. The whole thing happened so quickly. In 1985 I was the strongest man on board. In 1986 there was some pain. In 1987 I was lucky to get to the hospital alive... then months of rest, taking things slowly. Maria got on my nerves – I wasn't a bloody child, but she took control of everything. And the wheelchair, and I couldn't satisfy her anymore... But I made it! The day I got back to the ship and made those boxes move! Things had changed a bit though. We were no longer fishing, we were 'doing research' – and there were women! What would my father have said? But it was good, shifting boxes for them. Their perfume and their smiles and fat Maria at home! And then the English. Castration, and my mortality thrown in my face. ❑

DES DILLON

Someone Else's Tune

The bow is a bar
of ice melting on the warm strings
of bass and violins;
dripping the notes
into the air
humid
with the joys
and tears and little
fears that dance for now
to someone else's tune

Siesta

An old man meanders by dressed
for a Scottish winter.
The sun glints off the wine bottle
he grasps with monkey fingers.
Loose – in his left hand – six eggs.

He comes back unchanged
two hours later except for

the empty bottle and
the breeze in the fingers of his left hand,
the shadow of his cap on his forehead

and the group on Cocuruzzo square
has changed position but the same talk
whistles over the top of the slow swing of the bottle.

The Rosary Bell

The rosary bell
brings a stream of old women
in black along the ribbon of white dusty road.

Each is a walking Hail Mary.,
Our Father or Glory Be.
I can't tell if it's the prayers

or the walk or the bell that brought them
from cold shuttered rooms
and Mosquito nets in spring

They pass the giggling
jeans-factory girls like planets
in the wrong solar system.

They will float like virgins
into the endless space of religion
and silence might never touch them.

A factory girl gazes at the hills.

B MacKENZIE GARDINER

Jenners Tea

There is a changing room in Jenners that overlooks the Scott Monument. During the first week of the Edinburgh Festival, Miss Dolores Brown of Comiston has her hair done in Jenners and then shops for smalls. She always uses this changing room. With her careful selection of bras, panties, slips and handbags she waits for the room to be free. When her turn comes she closes the door and opens the curtains. The Monument is swarming but Sir Walter has eyes only for her.

She begins to strip, humming quietly to herself. She tries them all on for him, turning this way and that, dressed at times only in a handbag. He nods in stony approval of the ivory silk Dior. In all the years that Miss Brown has bought her smalls, in public at Jenners, no visitor to the Scott Monument has ever complained. Under Sir Walter's tutelage she has progressed from Damart to Dior, from cotton to lace, from January to August, from bashful to brazen, from 25 to 75. And what after all are national heroes for, if not to inspire the populace and entertain the tourists with the inside view of Scotland?

But not all of the populace have such an intimate relationship with Sir Walter as Miss Brown has. Take Bernice who has been seated beside Sir Walter for as long as Miss Brown has been in the lingerie department at Jenners. Bernice hasn't once glanced at the monument or at Jenners because she is nervously awaiting a certain Wottie with a glottal stop due off the 2.50pm train from Glasgow. Her gaze is fixed on the crowds entering Princes Street Gardens from the direction of the station. She doesn't know what Wottie looks like and that is exactly how her boyfriend has planned it.

'Sit on the seat under that monument and wait, he'll find you, ok?'

Wottie has a package which Bernice has agreed to transport to Fife. Nor does she know that Wottie has been told by her loving boyfriend to look for 'the fat tart in lycra and blue dreadlocks'. She glares at the crowds, a Doc Martened foot waving like a threat from the end of huge crossed shimmering legs. The tourists have steered clear of the bench on which Bernice is sitting. They don't mind getting to know men in skirts but big, big girls in purple lycra with petrol blue lips and matching hair are only readily approached by drunken males of their own nationality, or elderly ladies from Comiston flushed to the gills with the afterglow of shopping in Jenners.

Perhaps only Miss Brown, out of the entire population of Edinburgh, could have failed to notice Bernice sitting on the bench that afternoon. Certainly Bernice, lost in nervous anticipation of her biggest ever illegal act, fails to register any danger in Miss Brown and her Jenners bag settling in her proximity. The pigeons, showing no prejudice, approach them both hopefully, but receive no acknowledgement either.

The tourists are all happier now that Miss Brown and Bernice are sharing the seat next to Sir Walter with nothing dramatic befalling either of them. They began to loiter around the bench again, like the pigeons, and feel safe enough to view the monument since Miss Brown has proved that Bernice is benign.

Miss Brown, oblivious of passers by and hoverers, is drawing out the edge of the ivory silk Dior knickers to show to Watty. In moments of intimacy she does indeed call Sir Walter, Watty.

Carefully revealing a leg and a bit of gusset she says aloud, for she cannot help it, 'Well then Watty, what do you think of *these*?'

Bernice only hears the old dear muttering and sees her rummaging in her bag like any other bag lady. But Wottie, who has arrived breathless at the rendezvous, is only momentarily confused by the fact that Miss Brown's hair is definitely blue and she's just spoken to him. He has sampled the contents of his package and it has taken the edge off what few thought processes he has. He quickly realises how clever it is of his mate to have the fat tart as a decoy and the wee granny as the courier, so he sits down and answers Miss Brown with 'Very fuckin tasty' as he stuffs his hand and the package deep into her ivory silk drawers.

Miss Brown experiences something like a rapid descent from high altitude with three distinct shocks en route. The first one arises from having the f-word addressed to her, the second from the hand rummaging in her Dior underwear and the third from the fact that her Jenners bag is clutched particularly close to her bosom which is now also being manhandled by Wottie. Any one of these shocks would have been enough to render her speechless, but combined they render her immobile also, encouraging Wottie to believe he is on the right track. Bernice notices that the leering bloke is feeling up old granny further along the seat. She has a wee old granny in Fife who is the only human being who still accords her any respect and a deep anger stirs in the depths of her lycra.

'Ya fuckin perv,' she bellows and lunges at Wottie dragging him by the hair from out of Miss Brown's Jenners bag.

Something now stirs also in Miss Brown's depths. She is back in the blitz being manhandled by a Polish sailor and half a century of repressed rage fires up her limbs. A tourist who has been camcording the monument turns at the commotion and catches on film an elderly lady grinding her heel into the genitals of a prostrate male while a lycra clad valkyrie holds him down yelling 'Gie him it granny.' Miss Brown has never had such unfettered access to the private parts of a man and finds the act strangely satisfying. She stamps her anger into his groin with 'You... naughty... man.'

The tourists, like the pigeons, have started back in fear, but a passing drunk, seeing the action and the camcorder, fortuitously shouts out, 'Cut! Cut! That'll dae Ewan,' and a flock of Japanese visitors jump to the conclusion that they are witnessing Scottish art in the making. A young girl among them shrieks, 'Ewan Macgregor,' and soon the name is speeding around the crowd like wildfire. Bernice and Miss Brown are elbowed out of the way as a feeding frenzy develops on the moaning Wottie.

Bernice ushers Miss Brown safely on to Princes Street where she stops in front of Sir Walter seeking some reaction, but, sheepishly, his head is deep in his book.

'Well!' she mutters indignantly, 'men!'

'Too right,' says Bernice for she knows the problem only too well. The previous night her crotch had been grabbed in a Kirkcaldy pub by a big bloke wanting to know if she was a transvestite. With a fluttering tenderness Bernice halts a taxi for Miss Brown by leaping into its path and throwing up an arm. Just as she enters the taxi Miss Brown withdraws a pair of ivory silk Dior knickers from her bag and stuffs then into Bernice's hands. 'For you dear.'

Not being a transvestite, Bernice is not greatly taken with the gift, silk does nothing for her. When she returns to her spot the party is over. No Wottie ever arrives from Glasgow and she curses her boyfriend all the way back to Fife.

On arriving home, Miss Brown discovers an ornate tin marked Earl Grey Tea nestling among the remains of her Dior underwear, and taking it for granted that Jenners should reward a customer of her standing with a little pick-me-up she puts on the kettle and takes out her silver tea-pot.

In Jenners, the curtains are drawn back from a certain window and the wife of a distinguished Edinburgh barrister sees with dismay that Sir Walter's eyes are covered by what looks like a pair of discarded panties. ❑

TODD McEWEN

With Billy Collins in the Berg Room*

What words did not, wine and coffee told
on airmail tissues, the corners pinholed.
Lots of violet ink, violent scrawl and stink:
Kerouac's rainbow pads from markets on the road;
Auden's economical ledger sheets;
really it is all business here, as you think.

I'm sending you the third draft of;
Don't know if you can use;
Dear Mr Moss;
Can't be in America for a year or two.

Newsprint and yellow newsprint banged and harangued on;
Delmore Schwartz had a problem with his ribbon:
red invaded black and built him a ream of sorrow.
It was the Golden Age of Typewriting
and I will gladly pay you tomorrow.

Notebooks spill out of the desk at home
we are pleased to think are in no order
or in an order no one may catalogue thus.
Is the messy way the better to remember us?

Why write you a letter on one side?
Do I imagine my jokes pinned up in here like butterflies?

* The manuscript collection at the New York Public Library

SIMON CRUMP

Lady in Red

Elvis came out of the trailer which served as his dressing room on the set of the movie *Live a little, Love a little (drink a lot)*.

Chris De Burgh was waiting to see him, he'd been hanging about for ages, trying to get an autograph, and he was so happy to finally meet Elvis that the sad little man broke into song.

'A spaceman came travelling in his ship from afar, t'was light years of time since his mission, and over a village he halted his craft and it hung in the sky like a star, just like a star'

'That really was very poor,' Elvis said calmly.

'AM I SUPPOSED TO BE IMPRESSED BY THAT SHIT?' he screamed, then turned to me.

'Execute this reedy-voiced, ferret-faced little bastard NOW!'

It was pretty soon after the time when Elvis had been abducted by aliens and he was still very touchy about the whole topic of intergalactic space travel. He'd just been to see the film *Chariots of Fire*. He thought it was an Eric Von Daniken picture. One of Elvis's favourite books was Daniken's *Chariots of the Gods* and he'd hoped that the film version would help him come to terms with his own experience.

When he'd realised that it was about a faggoty bunch of English guys running around on a beach he went completely berserk and burned out the theatre. Which reminds me, when I catch up with him, that Colin Welland dude is sure gonna be sorry.

Anyway, so I twisted Chris's weedy arm up behind his back and marched him round the side of the trailer. I jammed the muzzle of my .38 in his mush and blammo! that little fucker wouldn't be dancing with the Lady in Red anymore.

That evening after the day's filming had ended, me and a few of the guys were sitting around with Elvis in his trailer, drinking tequila slammers and playing blackjack.

I heard this scratching sound coming from outside like there was a cat or a wild animal or something trying to get in. I opened the door a couple of inches and damn me if it wasn't Chris De Burgh back from the fucking dead.

His head was almost completely gone, there was a bloodied stump sticking out of his satin bomber jacket, but in a way he kinda looked a lot better, more human almost.

'Hey Guys!' I yelled, 'it's Chris De Burgh, back from the fucking dead!'

Anyway, I helped him up the little metal steps into the trailer. So, he's just stood there silhouetted in the doorway and we're all gawking at the empty space above his shoulders where by rights a head ought to be.

Suddenly this low booming voice like a 45 on 33 starts coming out of Chris's chest.

'Hey fellas, there's something I have to tell you, can I take a moment of your time?'

'Yeah, sure thing Chris baby,' we all say in chorus, like some dumb Sunday bible class.

'If you got something you need to share with us, then you go right on ahead.'

Frankly, I was a little worried, I'd wasted plenty of guys before, well obviously, it's kinda like a hobby to me, but Chris was definitely the first one who'd stopped by for a chat afterwards.

What if he wouldn't leave? It wasn't like I could blow his head off again or anything. Then I figured, 'I know, if he gets rude or nasty or bleeds on the rug or makes Elvis mad, I'll blow his legs off and shove his body in the trash.' So after that I felt a bit easier.

I got him settled nice and cosy on one of the folding canvas chairs which Elvis had ordered for all the Memphis Mafia when we got started in the movie business. I put a baseball cap over the stump coz close-up it was kinda unsightly and fixed the guy a drink.

So, he starts telling us what it is he needs to say. His diction seemed a little strange to me, but then I remember that the guy's English so that's probably why he sounds like such a fucking pansy.

'After eight years of pains I received the stigmata at the age of

31 on the 20th of September 1973; my wounds opened up and released a great deal of blood. For me as for many other stigmatics, my marks were very painful.'

'I had a vision about the time I recorded that great song *Don't pay the Ferryman...*' and his voice trails off like he's remembering the song.

At this point I can see the other guys are thinking about that song too, and they're getting angry and Elvis's face has gone a funny purple colour.

'Yeah anyway, Chris. Forget that dumb song, tell us about the vision,' I say.

'I saw before me a mysterious person. His hands and feet were dripping with blood. The vision disappeared and I became aware that my hands, feet and side were dripping blood. Imagine the agony I experienced and continue to experience almost every day. I am dying of pain from the wounds and because I like to wear white clothes and move about a lot on stage, I suffer from perpetual seepage-based, stain-oriented embarrassment.'

'Well, thanks very much for telling us about that Chris,' we all say in chorus again, then I take him outside and blow his legs off. ❏

August 1970

We went into Kerr's Sporting Goods one time and Elvis saw a real pretty .22. It was engraved and he bought it. Then in '70, he went in there on a spree and bought thirty two handguns, a shotgun and a rifle. That included a .44 Ruger Blackhawk gold-plated revolver which cost $1,850, and a .357 Colt Python revolver, which set him back $1,950. The total bill came to $19,792. Red's still got the receipt.

In the backyard at Graceland there's a big old lime tree and one late August afternoon in 1970, me, Elvis and my kid brother Red are using it for a spot of target practice. I'm using my navy issue colt, Red's got an M101 Duramatic pistol and Elvis is using his fancy fucking lah-di-dar gold-plated Blackhawk.

We've got beercans, Coke bottles and some teddy bears that the fans are always sending in for Elvis all set up in the branches and we're blasting away like it's going out of fashion. We take it in turns to go up a ladder and prop the stuff back in the tree while the other two guys reload and then off we go again.

Gladys staggers out on the back kitchen door to see what's going on . As per usual at this time of day, she's completely wasted on her favourite combo of diet pills and cheap wine. She asks Elvis if she can have a try, we all exchange 'OhmyGod' glances but he says, 'Yeah ok, sure thing mom, but you gotta set up the targets first.' So she totters across the lawn, slowly climbs the ladder and crouches in a fork in the branches where she starts setting up the cans and shit. Elvis puts fresh bullets into his pistol, turns to me and smiles, 'Now ain't that somethin,' he drawls, and for one awful moment I think maybe he's going to blow his mom away.

Just then there's this Godawful scream and Gladys comes crashing out of the tree, hits the deck with a thud, and starts thrashing around in the long grass at the edge of the lawn, all the while hollering like a stuck pig.

So we go charging across the lawn to where the drunken old bird is having her shit-fit and then we see that she's completely covered in ants, great big green motherfuckers. I reckon they must've smelt the alcohol on her while she was up in the tree and figured that she was lunch. Come to think of it Elvis claimed to have seen some huge ants a couple'a days before, but we thought it was just the usual drugged-up crap he's always talking. Anyway, right after we all stop laughing Elvis tears off his shirt and starts flapping it over his mom to scare the ants away, and me and Red make a run for the kitchen to fetch buckets of water.

When we get back she's quiet and Elvis is kneeling next to her. 'Too late Guys,' he says, 'she's gone'.

And boy was it too late, and Holy Shit was she gone. Them flippin' ants had eaten up just about every part of Gladys except her jewellery, her dentures and some of her hair.

Damnedest thing I ever saw. ❑

Stairway To Heaven

Elvis opened up the throttle and felt his brand new Jetstar surge forward along the runway. As he eased back the stick the plane's nose came up and the rumble of tyres on tarmac was replaced by the low whistle of wind across the wings and fuselage. He was airborne and he felt great. There was a dull clunk as the undercarriage folded away and Elvis tuned the radio to Country Roads FM. He punched in a course for Cleveland Ohio and hit the auto pilot switch. Then he cracked open a Pepsi and washed down a handful of pills.

A few months earlier when he was on tour, Elvis met Led Zepplin on the tarmac of L.A. International Airport. Elvis hated Led Zepplin. He called them 'long-haired British freaks'. He hated their music, he hated their lyrics, he hated their album covers, he hated the way they looked, he hated the way they talked. He despised everything they stood for. Elvis's stepbrothers David and Ricky Stanley aged 17 and 18, were along for the ride. Both huge Zep fans, they'd wear Led Zepplin Tee shirts just to annoy Elvis, and when they saw their heroes disembarking from a nearby plane they dragged Elvis over with them so they had an excuse to meet the band.

Robert Plant, Jimmy Page, John-Paul Jones and John Bonham all signed autographs for the two boys who by this time had entered their own private Heavy Metal Heaven, and as they stood talking, Elvis looked over at their jet.

'I like your 707.'

'Yeah?' said Robert Plant. 'We lease it from...'

'Oh?' Elvis interrupted. 'I *own* mine'. Robert looked a little surprised at this, but he let it go and there was a short embarrassed silence.

'My kid brothers tell me you guys are pretty heavy,' Elvis said, desperately trying to plug the gaping hole he'd just ripped in the conversation.

'Yeah, but not as heavy as you, you fat fuck,' replied Plant, trying to be funny, as only the British know how.

'Ok guys, that's it, we're leaving,' Elvis screamed and stormed back across the blacktop to his own jet. Then he cancelled the gig and took off for Memphis. The trip back was a nightmare, the plane lost an engine on takeoff, made a very rough emergency landing at an airport in Burbank and Elvis was forced to abandon the rest of the tour.

Convinced that Led Zepplin had sabotaged his plane, Elvis was now on his way to teach them a lesson.

As his jet approached the outskirts of Cleveland, Elvis switched back to manual control and returning the radio to 'Those Were The Days' FM, he cranked the volume up as high as it would go. Then, with the March of the Dambusters blasting away in his headset and all kinds of prescription chemicals coursing through his veins, he jammed the stick forwards. The plane plummeted to 500 feet and levelled out over the Jacobs Field baseball field where a Led Zep gig was in full force. By now Elvis was so excited that his whole body was quivering. It was the point in the show where the band leave drummer John Bonham alone on stage to perform his obligatory 20-minute solo. The Jetstar came in fast and low over the field and with trembling hands Elvis inched back the two small levers which operated the cargo doors. He'd loaded up the hold of the Jetstar with a large polythene garbage sacks filled with a mixture of pigs blood and food dye. Then he'd shat in them all for good measure. The doors swung open and the whole bloody, shitty payload slithered out into the skies of Cleveland, directly over the auditorium. The crowd roared with approval, Led Zepplin were acknowledged masters of spectacle and their audience not only expected them to deliver – each time it had to be bigger and better. Unfortunately for the massed heavy metal fans gathered below, several hours of high altitude flying had frozen the liquid-filled sacks into solid lumps of ice which shattered on impact. The result was total and instantaneous carnage. Shards of red ice ripped through the crowd carving out long bloody corridors all the way to the stage and at the high point of his solo the neatly severed head of a young woman bounced off John Bonham's snare and lodged itself inside the P.A.

As his plane climbed rapidly to five thousand feet Elvis was oblivious to what was happening below. He thought he'd just played the best practical joke in the whole history of practical jokes ever, and he was laughing like a demented hyena. Backstage, the band decided it was time to forget about love, peace and harmony for a while. So far the body count was estimated at 30 and rising by the minute, with a further 220 fans seriously injured. It was already the worst disaster in Cleveland since the river caught fire. Shouting above the wail of sirens and the throb of paramedic helicopters, a badly shaken Robert Plant began to make a few phone calls.

Darkness had fallen by the time an elated Elvis touched down in Memphis. As he drove his Lincoln back home from the airstrip he heard the dull 'crump' of what he recognised from his army days to be a parachute mine, exploding somewhere in the distance. As he swung the car off Elvis Presley Boulevard, through the music gates and up the gravel drive towards Graceland, Elvis thought that the house looked somehow different. Then he realised that the upper floors were gone. Just like his birthplace in Tupelo, Graceland was now a bungalow. The shattered trees of the Meditation Garden were festooned with clothing and broken chandeliers. Splintered furniture, and chunks of masonry littered the lawns.

Elvis found Ricky and David crouching in the bushes by the pool house. Both seriously injured, they weren't making much sense, but they managed to tell him that Priscilla was still inside the house. He raced towards the front entrance and pushing through the debris in what remained of the lobby, he started up the main staircase. He saw then that it was shorn clean away and that now the stairway just vanished into the starry heavens. Then something made him stop short.

Looking up, he saw Priscilla spreadeagled across the first flight. Her face, wide open from scalp to chin, had no connection with anything that Elvis had ever seen. ❏

BRIAN McCABE

spider

In a previous life, they say
I hanged myself
for winning a spinning contest
with Athene.

Lies.
In my mythology
there are no goddesses:
just me and my mate and my prey.

He'll do that dance again
with his eightsome-reeling legs
and secrete a sticky compliment
on the dark design of my web.

It's just an air-strainer, I'll say.

He'll look into my two rows of eyes
finger my silk with his pedipalps
and call me his Athene.
I'll clear my throat.

Arachne, I'll say.

To save time, I'll turn round
and advertise my abdomen.
He'll realise why he was born.
Then I'll eat him.

Sluiced in my juice,
he'll make a nutritious soup.
I may not be a goddess, but
I've still got my legs.

viceroy

The pattern on my wings is a complex
stained-glass window affair
but the message
is simple:

I am poisonous.

But I'm not. I'm aware
of the Monarch's reputation
and I trade on it. Why not?
Who want's to end up a snack
for a pernickety oriole?

It works: I'm ignored
more often than I'm devoured.

But now there are so many of me
the monarch is sometimes mistaken
for her tasty impersonator
and is eaten.

I say to myself:
whats another sick predator?

Then
I cross the sunlit clearing
between one milkweed and another,
as slowly as I dare
wondering which of my reputations
has gone before me.

OWEN O'NEILL

Shoulder Bit

The shoulder-bit that I dragged from the sodden
undergrowth of a holly tree was a wet, hard sycamore,
and it slipped away from me. Its bark covered in green
slime, I could see my finger marks, failure.

Exuberant, inside the noise of a plastic anorak,
Sweating, steaming, in the quiet veiled rain, I sat on a
cold stone and thought for a split second about my
Grandmother and piles. The wood was around me, and in me.

I knew that everything was here. Every colour and smell
and enemy and strength and weakness and love and death
and life and all the secrets. Every root to the sky and
the earth.

This was where the clean shirts and socks and shoes of
the mummys' boys came to fear. Once upon a time, deep,
in the dark dark forest. This was where it all started,
and finished.

I stared at the long slim sycamore, imagines it in
neatly cut blocks, stacked up and dried out by the side
of the gable like big cigarette ends waiting for the
clear blue woodsmoke, that was freedom.

I went at it, heard it suck at the mud as it came free,
A born again tree, torn limb from limb. It was mine and
I hauled it up the hill through foliage and barbed
branches that tore at my legs and bled them.

Exhausted, I lay on top of it, and felt its power.
I counted the rings, twelve, same age as me. I'll have
you! An hour later I threw it from my shoulder, a little
body wracked with pain, and bursting with pride.

All the family cheered as it thudded and slithered on
the concrete like a frozen snake. My Grandfather was
drunk and said it would take ten years to dry out. My
Mother elbowed him and said he would take twenty.

Aunt Jeanie said it was bad luck to cut down a sycamore
because they were graveyard trees and their branches were
the arms of the dead on All Souls Night. My brother said
it would burn like an iron bar. But my Father knew.

He smiled and shouted, 'Good man yourself! You're a tight
man.' He knew, that his coffin would be safe on my
shoulder. That when the time came, I wouldn't let him
down. I would be well able to do my bit. My shoulder
bit.

It Was Only Eleven O Clock

Found him lying on the broad
of his back.
Inside the ring he had made
for himself.

He had always told me that he'd
been born with extra skin on
his skull. Said it was his lucky
cap. I believed him.

The sky in his eyes. The shame was,
it was too early for this.
Where was the night that protected
such people.

Oh Daddy get up! Daddy please get
up! Come on Daddy please get up
please Daddy get up. Daddy! Get
up please... it's only eleven o clock.

Away you and enjoy yourself son. I'm
alright here, cumulus stratus, the best.
There's change in me jacket, take it,
take it all, go to the dance tonight.

So I did. Some who knew, watched and
understood, smiled even. Then there were
those who saw a young man robbing a drunk,
blatant as you like. In the High Street.
In the middle of the day.

And my father, his sense of humour still
intact started shouting. Help! Somebody
help me! The fucker's stealing me money
Help! Call the police! Help me!

IAN MACPHERSON

From the Journals of Fiachra MacFiach (vol xxiv):

Spat

A most amusing spat with little-known Scottish versifier Luther 'Thrawn' Jannett. Jannett spends much of his time 'fleeing from the redcoats' (*sic*) and lives in a highland cave on a diet of wild berries and methylated spirits. He was in Edinburgh for the annual book festival where his agent had booked him a room at the Cowgate Salvation Army hostel and arranged a series of lectures on the pavement outside the same building. I was fortunate enough to catch him in action before the police arrived. His theme? 'That Authors Who Are Named After Public Houses Have An Unfair Advantage Over The Rest Of Us'.

He's absolutely right, of course. On a recent trip to Dublin I was intrigued to notice that many of Ireland's most famous authors had just such a kick start. Sean O'Casey, the well-known author of light comedies about the civil war, is an interesting case in point. Named appropriately enough, after The Sean O' Casey, he grew up to carry the process further. Many of his most famous confections were also named after pubs.

In England, where I am presently based, the situation is less artistic than military. Where, for instance, would the Duke of Wellington be today without a comparable leg-up. In his case several legs up, there being a Duke of Wellington in every town in the country.

I was beginning to warm to Jannett in spite of his rambling delivery and insistence on endorsing his chosen tipple – I am implacably opposed to sponsorship in the arts – when his bleary gaze landed on me.

'You'll be that dour pseudo-Celtic establishment boot-sucker MacFiach,' he quipped.

No doubt he was referring to the fact that my life's work, *Deep Probings*, was currently in its third edition and had sold a majesterial seventeen copies, twelve of them, admittedly, to the present writer's mother. In the rarefied world of genius such a sales figure in the author's own lifetime borders on the commercial. I had, I admit it, some sympathy for his stance. Envy is breakfast, dinner and a late fish supper to the likes of Jannett. He washed it down with a swig of spirit.

'I,' I replied grandly, 'am he.'

'You,' he continued, 'are the worst culprit of the lot.'

I was stunned. The Fiachra MacFiach? The Deep Probings? I couldn't think of a single example of either. I put this to Jannett with some force.

'Oh, it's not the name with you. No, nor the title neither. It's the bloody lines.'

I was flabbergasted. Jannett's mind operated on the far side of insanity without doubt, but he appeared remarkably lucid and sure of his ground on this occasion. I requested an elaboration of his thesis.

'The first so-called verse in your alleged book,' he sneered.

'*Lines For Seamus Heaney*,' I replied proudly. 'What of it?'

'You'll ken the words.'

'I am capable of reciting all my work,' I replied grandly, 'requested or otherwise.'

'Mostly otherwise, I'll wager, unless it's yourself does the requesting. On this occasion, mind, *I'm* doing the requesting.'

By this stage a large crowd had gathered. Low types, mainly, but a sprinkling of genteel Edinburghers made it worth my while to excel myself.

'The gnarled tree,' I declaimed, *'explores*
The muddy field,
Its lecherous roots probing
The wet, brown clay
Like the gnarled and crackling fingers
Of a tough, old two-quid whore.'

'That's the one,' cried Jannett with his customary vulgarity, cutting across my flow. 'The Tough Old Two Quid Whore'.

The wild-eyed loon had lost me I'm afraid.

'What about it,' I asked.

'High Street, Perth,' he said. 'Next door but one to Pimps' Nite Klub. Ten to one you're a valued customer.'

At this stage I'd had enough of his slanderous drivel. I had never been to Perth in my life.

'I am not in the habit of frequenting public houses,' I attested, 'except,' I said, turning my attention to the crowd, 'in the case of my weekly poetry night. Camden High Street, Three guineas at the door. The Gnarled Tree.' ❏

On His Alcohol-Induced Amnesia

Imagine my shock when I woke one morning to find the following article parked neatly in my typewriter.

APOLOGY

My 800-page biography of the celebrated transexual poet Joseph 'Mary' Plunkett has been roundly criticised for concentrating on his sexuality to the total exclusion of any reference to his work.

The fact that he had possibly bedded the Welsh Male Voice Choir (baritone section), all ranks past Lt. Col. in the US Air Force and the entire General Synod of the Church of England – with the honourable exception of Rabbi David Horowitz, the mole – seemed important as my research progressed, but I see now that I was swayed by the mood of the times. He also wrote.

On page 467 I further suggest that he was traumatised when his mother joined a lesbian sect operating out of Oughterard sub post office (sadly now closed). I apologise to the sub post office sub post mistress for any distress I may have caused her and her family. The fact that they were stoned to death by an angry mob adds further to my growing belief that I should have concentrated on the work and not the steamy, best-selling but highly dubious hearsay evidence about his and his family's sexual peccadilloes.

Page 532; the line 'He enjoyed an incestuous relationship with his half-sister Mary 'Joseph'.' This, of course, is totally without foundation, as has been established in a celebrated High Court case. I have borne all costs, including a hefty tip to the clerk of the courts for expunging a reference to me as a 'third rate writer who thinks he's second rate, a talentless hack with delusions of mediocrity.' The case in question, and I apologise unreservedly to the plaintiff, established that Plunkett drew no enjoyment from the alleged relationship, that no such relationship in fact existed, that the woman in question was not in fact the half-sister of the above (or any fraction thereof), that they had never in fact met and that her name was Carmel.

It is perhaps understandable that publication had a profound effect on the subject's Aunty Eileen. My descriptions of her bi-annual visits to Bangkok, and their illicit nature, were well wide of the mark. A mild-mannered octogenarian with a love of God and the colour black, she ended her days as a recidivist, a shoplifter and a Kings Cross hooker with very few clients. Mea culpa.

The reaction of his brother Jesus 'Maria' was far worse. He threatened to kill me. Naturally enough I took this to be a passing fancy and laughed it off. But no. To prove the seriousness of his intent, Jesus 'Maria' took a pot shot at me from the roof of Clery's department store, Dublin –

fortunately I was in Carlow at the time – and strapped a bomb to my car which exploded early, killing only a coachload of passing bomb disposal experts. Sorry about that lads. By this stage I assumed Jesus 'Maria' had cooled off somewhat. Not a bit of it. He espoused Islam at short notice, with tragic consequences. It caused me to cancel a book signing in Tehran. Apologies to my many fans in that neck of the woods.

I again wish to reiterate my sincere apologies to the above. I have learned a valuable lesson and propose to apply same to the forthcoming no warts biography of W.B. 'Rowdy' Yeats. Yeats, now chiefly remembered for his wine lodges, achieved a brief notoriety in the 1930s when he was photographed in the arms of Accrington Stanley's reserve sweeper. He also scribbled a bit.

On the positive side it must be conceded that, drunk or sober, I write beautifully. But, and it's a big but, I have so far been unable to unearth a copy of the biography in question. I don't remember writing that either. At eight hundred pages, however, it must have been some binge. ❑

My Fundamental Friend

1. Fillum

I'm always getting phoned up to do film parts and I always turn them down. I find it bumps up my fee, but that's not the only reason. I'm simply not offered the right parts. Take my most recent experience. I was approached my a leading director to appear in a big buget dramatisation of a novel by a fellow Dubliner. Ever since the success of *Darby O'Gill and the Little People*, apparently, Hollywood has been keen to present a realistic portrait of we Irish.

I turned the director down politely but firmly, and that, as I thought, was that. But no. The writer of this vignette of proletarian high jinks was on the phone not five minutes later. He got straight to the point.

"Ja wanna be in me fuckin' fillum, ya jammy fuckin' cunt ya?"

"No," I replied, "I don't want to be in your film"

"Why fuckin' noh, ya horse's fuckin' arse ya?"

"I just," I said testily, "don't."

"You fuckin' be in me fuckin' fillum or I'll fuckin' box ya. Righ?"

"Certainly not."

"Ja noh like me fuckin' bewke or wha'?"

"Not paricularly. No."

"Why fuckin' noh?"

"It deals with an area of the city which I find, to be perfectly frank, rather fundamental."

"Funda fuckin' wha'?"

"Mental. Clontarf, now. *There's* a fit location for a novel."

"Wha'? Clon fuckin' *torf*? Clon fuckin' *torf*? Are ya fuckin' jokin' me or wha'?"

"I never joke about Clontarf. Now take, for instance, a family of middle class suburbanites. Father a member of the Royal Dublin..."

"Oh, the Royal Doblin, yeh? Excuse fuckin' me."

"The Royal Dublin Golf Club. Mother..."

"A fuckin' whore. Righ'?"

"Mother involved with several local charities. Including, if I may make so bold, The Presbyterian church bazaar."

"Jayzus! Fuckin' Prods! Now why de fuck didn't I tink a dah? Fuckin' brillo! Janey fuckin' mack! Amn't I de righ' fuckin' stupid bollix? Fuckin' Prods. On'y everyone else is a fuckin' Katlick. Righ'?"

"That is substantially correct."

"So de fuckin' Proddy dawther has a fuckin' snappah. Righ'?"

"Snapper?"

"Ya know. Chizzler."

"I'm sorry. I don't quite comprehend."

"Jayzus. She has a fuckin' babby. Righ'? On'y she's on'y fuckin' six. So de fuckin' Da says, 'Righ'! Which one a youze Katlicks is

afther bangin' up me fuckin' dawther yiz shower a fuckin' cunts yiz?'
So de fuckin' Katlicks says, 'De whole fuckin' lor of us ya Proddy
fuckin' fuck ya.' So de Proddies geh some ammo an' de Katlicks geh
some ammo an' before ya fuckin' know ih de Katlicks is knockin' the
shihe owa de Proddies. Righ'? Annyway, de fuckin' Rewskies an' de
Yanks... Nah. Hold fuckin' on. A bih pa-fuckin'-say pardon me fuckin'
French. No. Dah cunt in de fuckin' Gulf pokes 'is fuckin' conk in an'
before ya know ih, Arma-fuckin' -geddin. Fuckin' Romeo an' Julieh
eat yar fuckin' bollix ouh. Fuckin' brillo!

"Ja wanna be in de fuckin' fillum?"

GLOSSARY OF TERMS
Dramatisation Takin' all de stuff owa de bewke where no-one's
fuckin talkin'.
Darby O'Gill and the Little People Fillum made fuckin' ages ago
by some fucki' cunt who's prob'ly dead now. If 'e isn't 'e soon fuckin'
will be.
Vignette Word used by some amn't-I-de-righ-poncy-fuckin'-cunt
type a shihe.
Proletarian Cunts like you an' fuckin' me. (Sic)
Presbyterian Presboes are sorta failed fuckin' Prods."
Bazaar "I tink it's like if ya see somethin' that's a bih fuckin' weird,
like. 'Jayzus!' ya say 'Fuckin' bazaar or wha'?' " ❑

2. Grewpe

I met my fundamental friend in the flesh today. Still exercising
his muse, I'm afraid. Music, this time, or what passes for same
with today's youth. I was minding my own business as usual. It
being Sunday, I was perusing Saturday's *Irish Times* and partaking
of a solitary glass at my local hostelry when the peace of the
Sabbath was shattered.

"Ja waana be in me fuckin' grewpe, ya horse's fuckin' arse ya?"

Needless to say, I had no intention of becoming involved in his
latest project.

"The last time we had the pleasure of meeting," I replied, "you were involved, as I recall, in the cinematic as distinct from the musical arts."

"Fuckin' mugs game, tha'. Crowd a cunts ouh in Holyhead."

"Wood."

"Hoh?"

"Hollywood."

"Fuck. Holly-fuckin'-wood! Jayzus! Amn't I de righ' stewpah fuckin' bollix? Thar eck-fuckin'-splains ih."

"Explains what, may I venture to ask."

"First fillum fucker I meh, he tore me bag ta fuckin' bihs an' fucked me back on the fuckin' mail bohe."

"Shocking way to treat an artist," I commiserated. "Small wonder that the Holyhead film industry is in terminal decline."

"Fuckin' spor on. Annyway, ja wanna be in me fuckin' grewpe or fuckin' noh?

"Certainly not."

"Ah, come *on*. It's fuckin' so-el."

"So-el? And what, pray, is so-el."

"Fuckin' Wilson fuckin' Pickehh. Oris Reddin'. Clarence Frogman fuckin' Henno."

"Not my style, I'm afraid."

"Wha'? Wha'? Yor nor a fuckin' jazz boy, are ya?"

"Tut tut no. Dear me no. Arid stuff. Atonal."

"Ya mean fuckin' shihe. Lissen.

"WHAYUN A MAYUN LEURVES A WERMAYUN JUNKA JUNKA JUNKA JUNK..."

At this point three gentlemen at the bar looked over. It was difficult to gauge their precise level of enjoyment – balaclavas do tend to transmit an aura of ambivalent mystery – but my fundamental friend seemed in no doubt as to the critical nature of their collective gaze.

"Whar a youze cunts lookin' ah, yiz cunts of a shower a cunts?"

The gentlemen thus addressed appeared unperturbed by the aggressive nature of the above line of questioning. They merely laughed drily and continued fondling their Spritzers. They left shortly afterwards. Nor, I felt, without some earnest sidelong glances at my fundamental friend, who was by this stage exorcising his musical demons at the bar.

"SAY IH LOW-ED," he bellowed, "HNH!

EYEM BLACK BUR EYEM PROW-ED. HNH!"

I was about to disabuse him of this rather fanciful notion when it suddenly struck me who the gentlemen in the balaclavas actually were.

"You ill-mannered nincompoop," I admonished. "Don't you realise who those illustrious gentlemen were?"

"Course I fuckin' do ya lard-arsed gobshite. De fuckin' Provos. So fuckin' wha'?

"SIRRIN IN DE MOANIN' SEURN

EYE'LL BE SIRRIN WHEN DE EVE-A-NIN CEURMS.."

"Not so," I ejaculated with passion. "*Not* the Provisionals, Sir. The Batchelors!"

"WATCHIN' DE..."

He was, I am surprised to report, momentarily struck dumb.

"De fuckin' Bachelors?"

"The Bachelors," I repeated, savouring the moment.

"Noh de fuckin' Bachelors?"

"The."

"As in Smy-el for me my Di-fuckin'-ane?"

"The same," I replied. "Incognito, of course."

"Fuckin' fuck!"

"Indeed. You can't expect them to just, as it were, stroll about the place. Not after the heights they've reached. Good God, man! The fans would tear them to bits."

"Fuckin' fuckin' fuck fuck fuck."

He seemed preoccupied, and moved towards the exit shaking his neanderthal head in a passable imitation of sorrow. Outside, I noted, the close harmony popsters were waiting to offer him a lift home. No hard feelings they seemed to be saying. Anyone can make a mistake. But as he went to join them my fundamental friend was still overcome by remorse.

"De fuckin' Batchelors," he concluded as the public house door swung shut. "If the fuckin' Mammy finds ouh she'll fuckin' kill me."

A somewhat over-heated response to a genuine misunderstanding, some might feel, but I have to report that I have not laid eyes on on the same gentleman from that day to this. So perhaps she did.

GLOSSARY OF TERMS

Cinematic arts Fuckin' fillums.

Holyhead Okay okay. So I fuckin' bewbed. No need ta go fuckin' on abower ah.

Jazz boy A fuckin' jazz boy for fuck's sake.

Commiserated Took de fuckin' piss.

Arid Fuckin' shihe.

Atonal Fuckin' shihe. De fuckin' English langwidge is full a fuckin' words dah jus' mean fuckin' shihe. I mean why don't yiz jus' say fuckin' shihe.

Neanderthal Fuck knows. Fuckin' huge word, buh. ❑

DUNCAN MACKAY

Bravehert

YOU MAY
sit here hen
if ye dinnae
waant tae sit
at the aisle
Ken
disnae boather
me wan wey or
the ither
Ah kin ayweys
stretch ma legs
oot if ah sit
ther

TAKE
sum poapcorn
Ah'll nivver
eat aw that
on ma ain
Ah dinnae
eat much
like
wance ah'm
ingrossed in the
pictur
like

OUR LIVES
wid be a lot
easier

if ma seat
didnae snap
shut ivry
time ah move
That's twice ah've
pooked ma stockins
oan it
Ah cannae afford tae
splash oot
oan a new pair
wi ma pension

BUT YOU WILL
like this bit
hen
They aw pull
up thair kilts
an show
thair bits tae
the inglish
It'll appeal
tae you
bein young
an that
Ah ken whit
young yins are
like these days
Ah ken

NEVER TAKE OUR
wey ay life
fur grantit
It cuild aw
backfire
an
we wid be

lik Wullie
Wallace
an aw
his wee freens
fechtin the
inglish
wi bits ay
auld stick
an
an arra-heid
Ay
youse
young yins
might
think yer
life's hell
bit a bet
if ye wur
pit back a
few years
ye widnae
last fur lang

TAKE OUR
polis
fur example
Ah mean
thai're
aw shoutin aboot
waantin tae
cairry
guns'n'that
Thai widnae ken
whit tae dae
wey
a sword

or a bit
spear
wid thai?
Oh hen
is that
the end
ay the
filum
awready?
An here's me
gabbin awa
Weel it wis
awfie nice tae
speak tae ye
Ah'll awa nou
an gie ye
peace
Ah might be
auld bit
ah ken how youse
young yins
like yir

FREEDOM

Blootert

Seik
    Stupit hoor wis seik
    aw oor thi
    flerr
    ower thi tap ay a
    blanket
    an intae a fukkin
    pint gless
Puke
    An it didnae
    feenish therr
    next tae git it wis the
    kitchin sink
    wher it wis left
    tae
    go aw hard an
    attract bluddy
    flees
Voamit
    Ah huv tae hand it tae ur
    mind ye
    efter aw that
    she still hud enough ay
    ur dinner left tae
    spew
    doon thi lavvy
    an aw up
    thi wa
    an no forgettin
    thi pile left
    blockin thi
    drain at thi back
    step
Coupit
    Bit naw

she didnae clean it up
she jist fell intae bed an
it wis forgoat aboot
till moarrnin
when seikness is thi
last thing that onybudy
waants tae see
an even the thought o it
gies ye thi bowks
an the only person
that disnae ken
whaes seik it is
is hur
Lyin shite
Bit naw
it couldnae hae
been hur
she's never seik when shes
pished
she jist talks a lot
It must hae been me
Aye me –
that goat lipstick on
the toilet seat
that left a pair ay
frilly knickers at thi
back door efter
wipin ma mooth
oan thum
that hud Linda
McCartney's tofu bluddy
treats fur ma dinner
Aye
it must hae been me

Ah'm fukkin sure it wisnae!

IAN RANKIN

Acid Test

There was no great excitement when the body was first discovered.

It had been found during excavation work beneath Old College. Fire prevention: they were installing a new sprinkler system, requiring the construction of a water-holding tank in the bowels of the quad. As one undergraduate had been heard to mutter: 'Waste of money. Long time since heat was generated in this place.'

'He meant intellectual heat, of course,' Professor Sandy Gates explained to Inspector Rebus.

'Of course,' Rebus said.

They were in one of the tunnels that ran beneath Old College, probably with James Thin's bookshop somewhere above them. The skeleton had been found there, covered with a thin layer of earth and rocks. And though the story had generated only a couple of paragraphs on one of the *Scotsman*'s inside pages, there was interest among the university academics along with a certain amount of bickering over territory. The archaeologists were claiming the skeleton as their own, while historians wagged their fingers and shook their heads. The lawyerly figures in Old College had a case of their own to offer.

But for now, it had been decided, the whole collection of bones and dust should be left in the hands of Professor Gates. And of course there had to be police involvement, too, at least until it could be established that there had been no foul play.

'Not my sort of thing,' Rebus said, kicking at a stone. Arc lamps had been set up by the workmen, and threw huge spiralling shadows over the vaults.

'There are miles of these tunnels, you know,' Gates said. 'Didn't realise there were any here though." He paused, looked around. 'This is the spot.'

The skeleton had been exhumed, photographed and removed to the pathology lab. As head of the pathology department, Gates had no intention of letting anyone but himself examine the remains. He crouched down, one hand on the ground to help balance his huge frame.

'One thing,' he said. 'Not much in the way of clothing. A few scraps of some blue material.'

'Think the rest perished?'

Gates shrugged. Depends how long the poor devil was down here.

'Your best guess?'

'A hundred, maybe two hundred years. The cloth's gone for analysis.' He glanced up at Rebus. 'We probably won't be able to narrow it down to a date and time.'

Rebus smiled. 'Then let's hope there's no need for a murder inquiry.'

'But?'

'But seeing how we're dealing here with a miscreant who'll never be caught or tried, and probably never identified in the first place, I'd make the assumption that our friend here met an unnatural death. And poison would be my guess.'

Rebus was thoughtful for a moment. 'So what now?'

'You're making it your business?'

"Unlawful killing, Professor. Can we get a fix on the deceased's age at time of death?"

Gates nodded. 'Dental forensics can do wonderful things. I'll remove a tooth or two for analysis. He turned to his colleague. 'And meantime we wait?'

'We wait,' Rebus agreed.

They waited. The world turned, and fresh cases filled their days. A stabbing, a suicide leap. Rebus had a few domestics to sort out, a court case to attend. After giving his evidence he bumped into Professor Gates.

'The McMurdo case?' Gates guessed. Rebus nodded. Gates explained that he'd already given his own evidence.

'Any progress with Piltdown Man?' Rebus asked as they walked from the High Court.

'A little. The scrap of cloth yielded something. Its age for one thing. Best estimate is mid-nineteenth century. The material is cotton, maybe underwear of some kind. Long johns or whatever they wore back then.

'So he was buried in just his underpants?'

'An educated guess, I believe. From the tooth, we're talking about an age anywhere between mid-teens and mid-twenties.

'So a student rather than a lecturer.'

'Or someone from outside.'

An outsider who knew about those tunnels?'

'Ah, but only the killer needed to know.'

Rebus chewed his lip. 'True.'

'Maybe there was work going on. One of the workmen at the time...?'

'Buried in just his underwear?

'To make identification more difficult.'

They were outside now. The day was clear and sunny, the buildings radiant. Office workers were out hunting for lunch.

'The other clothing couldn't just have disintegrated?' Rebus asked.

Gates shook his head. 'We'd have found buttons, some fibres.'

Gates nodded. 'Witness statements could be a problem.' He paused. 'Unless you have a ouija board handy.'

Rebus was pointing to a section of the wall. 'Is that it?'

'That's it,' Gates confirmed. The reason they were down here: the writing on the wall. Rebus held a torch close to the scratch marks. Even so, they were barely legible.

'Someone had sharp eyes.'

'Wish I could take the credit,' Gates said. 'But it was one of the workmen.'

'You think the writing connects with the body?' Rebus ran the torch over the wall seeking more clues.

'Judging by position, I'd have to say yes. The scratches are less than a foot from where the corpse's hand was uncovered.'

'Rebus looked again. Four capital letters, spelling out the word ACID.

'What's acid got to do with it?'

The two men were in the pathology lab. It hadn't been thought necessary to transfer the skeleton to the mortuary – there'd be no post-mortem in the usual sense. The bones had yet to be cleaned, though samples of bone and soil had been sent to one of the specialist labs.

Professor Gates shrugged at Rebus's question. 'Intriguing though isn't it?.' He pointed to the skull. No signs of damage or injury.' Ran his hand down the rib-cage. 'No obvious breaks or fractures. Nothing consistent with a violent demise.'

'Doesn't mean he wasn't killed.'

'You're thinking poison?'

'Or acid, something that would strip the skin away.'

'Hmm.' Gates sounded unconvinced.

'What else could the message mean?'

'I agree it's unlikely our friend died from natural causes. Looks to be the skeleton of a young adult male. Probably a fairly healthy specimen. Look at the teeth: they're intact. Others know more about the history of dentistry than I do, but I'm willing to bet if he'd been poor or malnourished, teeth would have been missing.'

'Well, whatever happened to him, someone buried the body.'

'But that might that not have been later. Maybe to avoid a scandal.'

'What sort of scandal?'

'Corpses found on college property – hardly a good advertisement. Could be he committed suicide.

'In a tunnel? It's an unlikely setting.'

Gates sighed. 'You know me, John. I'm not given to speculation. And if this were a contemporary case, I'd hold my tongue...'

'Who made those scratches? The victim, right?' Gates merely shrugged. 'Let's assume it was. What would he be trying to tell us?'

'The identity of his killer?'

Rebus nodded. 'But the body was buried.' They'd stopped walking. Pedestrians around them, catching snatches of conversation, turned their heads to stare. 'The body had to be buried *after* the scratches were made.'

'You have a theory?' Gates half-smiled. He guessed Rebus had been busy late into the night, thinking the case over.

'The body's left in the tunnel. Then the killer thinks better of it, and comes back to bury it. He doesn't want it found. Maybe he removes the clothing at the same time.'

'But is too delicate to remove everything?'

Rebus nodded. 'Someone with a shed of decency. But here's my point... between times, the victim wasn't quite dead. There was enough spark for him to pick up a stone and scratch a message.'

'And the killer didn't see it?'

'By candlelight, no. It was hard enough with arc-lamps and torches.' He looked to Gates, who nodded agreement.

'Which leaves us not a great deal more enlightened,' the pathologist added. The he saw the twinkle in Rebus's eye. 'Except you've done a bit more digging.'

But Rebus shook his head. I'm no archaeologist, Sandy.' He pause. 'But I know someone who is.'

Which wasn't strictly true. Meg Gilfillin was no archaeologist, but she *was* the university's archivist. Rebus visited her in a third floor office in Buccleuch Place.

'I've been following the story,' she said, peering over her glasses. There were three desks in the room, each covered with maps, plans and newspapers. She'd lifted a pile of bulging folders from a chair so that Rebus could sit down.

'Fascinating,' she said, looking at him as though he were the object of her studies. 'Your phone call was spot on. There was building work going on at Old College for a good part of the late 1880s.' She saw the look of disappointment on Rebus's face. 'Doesn't help narrow things down, does it?'

'No.'

'But this might.' She slid a photocopied sheet towards him. It was a page from the *Scotsman*, dated February 12th 1877. There was a story, one long narrow column, concerning some artefacts found in a tunnel under Chambers Street. The artefacts – jug, utensils, wine bottles – were thought to date back to the seventeenth century. Rebus looked up at her. She was nodding.

'The problem,' she said, is that from the evidence of this, not many people in Edinburgh wouldn't have known about those tunnels.'

Rebus passed the information on to Professor Gates, then prepared an interim report, stating that as far as a solution was concerned the Procurator-fiscal's office might as well forget it. A press release was issued, and barely taken up by the media.

The story, such as it was, had died.

Ten days later, Rebus received an invitation from Professor Gates to meet him at his office. The view from Gates's window was of McEwan Hall and Teviot Row. Rebus, whose own meagre view from the CID suite at St Leonard's was of the cop-shop car park, gazed out at another perfect late-spring day as he waited for Gates.

The pathologist bustled in with a grunt of apology and set his weight down on an antiquated swivel-chair, motioning for Rebus to be seated, too.

'I'm grateful you lot haven't been keeping me too busy,' Gates said. 'Given me a chance to do some detective work of my own.'

'Oh?'

Gates searched in his drawers for a folder, drew it out and slapped it onto the desk. He tapped it as he spoke. 'Poison and students, John. Students with a knowledge of poisons.'

'Medical students?'

Gates nodded. 'There were some great men in the medical faculty. Lister, Bell and the rest. It was a time of experiments and research, great finds. Mind, they weren't always successful. The first guinea-pigs to try laughing gas... there were near fatalities.' He stared at Rebus.

'Accidental poisoning?'

'Think for a moment. A group of students, doing their own work or just playing silly beggars. Testing cocktails of drugs. It happened then as now.'

'What's in the folder?'

Gates smiled at Rebus's impatience. 'Let's say one of their number dies, or seems to be dead. Maybe they can't find a pulse. They see their whole careers crumbling, even before they've begun. So what do they do?'

'Hide the body,' Rebus stated.

'Precisely.'

'But what about the acid?' Rebus asked.

Gates opened the folder, slid out photocopies: old faculty records. 'I was glad Miss Gilfillan came up with that news cutting. It narrowed my search. In 1877, there were a dozen students training with particular emphasis on pathology. One of them was called John Candless. This is the faculty roll for 1877.' He pushed the sheet towards Rebus. 'Three years later, the students graduated. But Candless wasn't amongst them.' This second sheet he now pushed towards Rebus, who was nodding agreement.

'No one,' the pathologist went on, 'seems to know what happened to Candless. I've found what records I can, and it seems he just vanished into thin air as far as the university was concerned.'

'Our skeleton?'

'Possibly.'

Rebus studied the sheets. 'We'll never prove it.'

'No. But let's take the game a little further.'

Rebus sat back in his chair. There was excitement in Gates's eyes.

'Another medical student,' Gates continued. 'He set up as a consulting pathologist around 1877. By 1880, he was far from his *alma mater*, working on a whaling ship.'

He leaned forward in his chair. 'The writing on the wall, John.

That capital I, fainter than the other letter.' He pushed the photograph towards Rebus. 'What if it's not an I? What if it was meant to be the downstroke for the D, only the author didn't think it was deep enough, so tried again?'

Rebus blinked. 'ACD?' He looked again at the graduation list. His finger tapped the name.

Gates was nodding, leaning back now, hands together as if in prayer.

'He covered up the mishap, hid the body, then returned to give it more of a burial. Guilty conscience perhaps. Maybe he had his own way of dealing with that dark secret in later life. Maybe it never left him...'

Rebus saw at last. The sheet fell from his hand. 'ACD,' he said. 'Arthur Conan Doyle.'

Gates applauded silently. 'Elementary, isn't it?' he said with the merest ghost of a smile. ❑

EDDIE GIBBONS

Bloke

When the work dried up I took to drink.
I pissed my family down the sink.
I left my wife, or she left me,
The kids survive on charity.

It's one for the pain and two for the road.
I'm shifting shit by the lorryload.
I trowel it up and I dish it out:
Once with my fists and twice with my mouth.

I hail a cab with a one pound note
And ride until the meter's broke.
The taxi driver wins the chase
And takes his fare out of my face.

Now it's cold on the road at two o clock.
There's blood on the ice where I took my knocks.
I'm down on my luck and down on my knees,
The snow in my shoes is starting to freeze.

I crawl to the door and I stab at the lock.
My hands are frozen into blocks.
I'm dumb in the heart and numb in the head.

It's a thousand stairs up to my bed.
These nights on the ale and days on the dole
Soak through your skin and sink your soul.
Fags and whisky make me choke.
I'm broke as a bloke with a hole in his coat.

When the work dried up I took to drink.
I pissed my money down the sink.
My suicide's such a lazy crime:
I'm drowning myself one glass at a time.

Icks

Grimerick

Looking surprised and taken aback, he
felt the gore of his face turning tacky
when a shot from the Knoll
shook him like a rag doll
in that limo in Dallas with Jackie.

Limberick

There was a young airman named Bader
who pushed to the limits, then harder
Though legless, this ace
would never lose face,
and he smashed Hitler's airborne Armada.

Limerick

A mistress named Monica L.
went down with her boss rather well.
Havana good time
isn't a crime
but removing the stains can be hell.

LUCY ELLMANN

Apple Pie & Barbecue

Each *apparently* the apple of his eye, if his first choice doesn't come to anything, someone else will fit the bill. His desire isn't generated by specific women, it's an overflowing thing that finds various eddies. Once he moved on to the next gal but he was too fast – the first one wanted him after all! So now, through no fault of his own (merely an overabundance of need and response to need) he has THREE women, all equally dependent on his love and convinced of his FIDELITY. Each apparently the apple of his eye. Apples hang heavy in October: keeping all these women happy was an impossibility. In fact it was a good excuse for keeping NO woman wholly happy. They got their fractions, their slices of pie – apple pie! – and had to make do with that. His multitudinous responsibilities included WORK as well as women (who were *sometimes* work), friends, relatives, DOGS, (his wife had decided to breed huge gangly wolfhounds). Actually, he had reached the stage where he could not caress a *breast* without his loyalties being divided.

Like a lot of morally uncertain men, he was an expert on good behaviour in women – he was certain about what THEY ought to be doing. There's nothing quite like your adulterous lover telling you to CALL YOUR FATHER, TIDY UP, or DEAL WITH YOUR CHILD. He was a useful addition to any household. Or – an addition anyway.

Like a lot of men, his ego was much bound up with owning a computer. If he really liked a woman, he offered to install his computer in her place.

Nonetheless, there's something to be said for the fastening together of genitals. His cock so neatly slotted into a variety of cunts. So well perhaps that no single woman fully deserved him – they HAD to share. He was splendid in his way.

HIS EX-WIFE'S VIEW:

He was the kind on man who finds fault with everything. He was forever taking his HI-FI to some repair shop way out in WATFORD – by TRAIN – when there was NOTHING WRONG with it. He found fault with things you'd never thought of! When he was in a hurry once to catch the train to Watford, I asked him if he needed anything and he said a TANGO. So I rushed through the station to get him a Tango, got back breathless just before the train left, handed him the Tango through the window and he *frowned*. 'It's not cold,' he said. I apologised, tried to explain that there WERE no cold ones. He said he'd save it for later. And off he went to his fucking hi-fi warehouse repair-shop depository. That's how it was, *my* disappointment just one step behind his. NO ONE could keep up with him; he was hard-done-by *par excellence*. I failed him repeatedly. The only reason he liked me was that there were so many things wrong with me.

HIM & HIS GIRLFRIEND:

Insatiable, her need for love, human touch, sex, food, booze. She tells him that despite his charm and her love for him, she fears he will never be able to appease her need for attention, affection, whatever. He thinks it over and one day sits her down, says he will not leave her side until she asks him to. He stays with her, looks at her, chats to her, holds her hand, clasps her, follows her to the loo, gently fondles her all night in bed, never lets her not feel his touch, his presence. When she's sick of the sight of him he leaves but returns with bags brimming. He cooks and cooks and makes her eat and eat until she can eat no more, still he makes her eat though. When she's full and fat he goes out again and returns with two litres of gin, with which he makes her MARTINIS day and night. She becomes aggressive after two but he keeps making them until she learns to drink FOUR at a time without passing out. On waking he makes her more and when she is drunk and floppy he fucks her for hours. When he's tired he fucks her with dildos, for hours and hours and hours.

She becomes contented.

The end.

THE WHOLLY IRRELEVANT YEAR OF THE BARBECUE:

There are events that CHANGE LIVES. For me, it was the arrival of a barbecue joint in my home town when I was about ten. I'll never forget the taste of that stuff, which we all liked SO MUCH at first. My family and I ate so much barbecued stuff from the barbecue joint that it colored that whole year for me. For us all! The whole town! (The whole town SMELLED of it.)

The barbecue joint just seemed to appear one day, a whole new building was built for it, big heavy wooden logs and almost instantly the big heavy wooden smell of MEAT everywhere, meat covered in their own particular unforgettable brand of barbecue sauce. Just opened up one day smelling interestingly of barbecue sauce, enticed everybody in town in there to eat barbecued food with that barbecue sauce all over it all year long, FILLED the town with that distinctive smell and the tell-tale takeaway dishes and the scraps of fried potato all over the sidewalk outside, old gnawed ribs in the gutter, fed EVERYONE in town faithfully for a full year until everyone was SICK of it, sick to death of barbecue, the distinctive smell of THAT particular barbecue sauce, sick of the THOUGHT of it, and then the place closed down, just like that!! (Lack of trade!) This is what people DO. They take you up, embrace you, force their barbecue sauce on you, ENVELOP you in this essence of their being, and then drop you full to the brim with barbecued meats, RUINED by the THOUGHT of barbecued meats, OVERCOME by their dose of Americana wafting all round your nice home town that never

ASKED for a barbecue joint, never *knew* about barbecue joints until that particular barbecue joint APPEARED out of the blue one day and FILLED the place with that SMELL, that taste, those particular thick french fries you'd never seen or IMAGINED could *be* so thick before. Closed down, just like that.

Don't you see? There's no knowing exactly how that barbecue joint, that barbecue taste, that barbecue smell and that barbecue eventual FAILURE affected everyone in town. BUT IT MUST HAVE. ❑

DAVID TOMASSINI

Fragments for a Venetian Epic

A man must work to some end – Joseph Conrad

Reminder

A sudden slap of the swollen waters:
a glistening boat's ropes
rub at the pier.
Drab, dilapidated spirit
in this sea-black night,
you sense the time is near.

Captain

Twisted temperament or perverted times?
Alone through necessity – his.
A psychic convulsion making him,
breaking him, pushing him on.
We'll follow.

Crew

Swiftly moving through the mist,
they leave no trace behind.

The boats they left have now chugged off,
churning in with deep sea sounds.
Above them all San Giorgio's bell rings clear.

Navigator

The hag's hair hung from the sky.
The streets echoed with his songs
as glaze-eyed he gazed
at the drug-glass green sluggish canal.
'My mistake,' he juggled with his hurt,
'I made you in my own image:

the rising figure on the bridge
wasn't you and you another too,
not the rush of love that rose
to greet the figure on the bridge.'

At least he's ready,
full of emptiness.

Engineer

Happy shavings, whistling steam,
spinning spokes, canvas's folding fall.
And then oil, sweat, stench...
A bare turbo turns, gleams in the dark;
he hums a rocking-horse rhyme
and smiles at the thought:
his daughter astride and singing.
Eight bells, full fathom,
without hope or despair,
he lives in the belly
with his tacit knowledge,
his engine room ego.

Where, When...

Half-owre, half-owre
This our lost life
We're bound for the rio
We can't settle down
for little things.
Machine mastering men
we have to look beyond,
delineate infinity.

But circular time locks our soul
from darkness to light
to dark again,
we're never ready to go.
The rigging is taut,
our charts lie empty
and the compass spins in vain.

A Maitter o' Scale

Oor universe smeared oot on a bit gless,
God peers doon his manoscope
an' is fair dumfoonerit tae see his sel
– Jings, A'm A made up o' aw i' thaim?

Doon on the bit gless man is birling roon
Trying tae catch a' haud o' his bacterial
tale. DNA. That's the stuff, the code
for sending messages tae oorsells.

It's aw a maitter o' scale. Oor universe
but an atom in the dirlin affairs o' God.
Aye, an' whaever's hauding the godoscope
maun be skartin his muckle heid!

DILYS ROSE

Flesh and Blood

Arlene: As much as he could use the word of her, he was impressed that she'd stuck out camping in Boon's dingy, stuffed-to-the-gills basement for so long. If she and her author had any sense, they'd have sloped off to his hotel. But Frankie boy was American and maybe fucking in the bowels of the old town, bang up against some historical gore could have one hell of a turn-on. The tourist industry thrived on ghost sightings and tales of dungeons and desecrated graves, houses of correction and of ill-repute, body snatchers and plague pits. All were exhumed and embellished daily for the edification of drop-jawed school children and snap-happy Japanese tourists:

> Here is where Burke and Hare drank and hatched plans to bump off their unlucky victims. Here where doctors exchanged cash for flesh and no questions asked. Here X had his throat cut, here Y was strangled, poisoned, garrotted, bludgeoned, hacked, stabbed, run through, shot, hung, drawn and quartered. These are the bloodstains, this is the weapon, here where the condemned man ate his final meal, here a Styrofoam replica of what he ate. Here the ghosts of dismembered corpses are reputed to have danced the night away, scaring a family from Iowa out of their mid-west wits. Here. plague victims were walled in and left to die; it's said you can hear their cries of protest most clearly on windy nights. Here, a fourteen year old girl submitted to her breasts being milked by one or more members of the kirk session as

proof of her licentiousness, the blackness of her soul. Here, during a time of famine, a starving mother sold her first born as butcher meat. Here, a lonely crone was alleged to have been seen fornicating with the devil. Here, she was burned at the stake for the same. Here, a man accused of fornicating with a goat was hanged. The goat was hanged on the same scaffold. The wax tableau illustrates the massacre of a clan, an early example of what would now be called ethnic cleansing. This, Scotland's last queen, on orders from her English rival, is about to have her head chopped off. This, an infamous family of highway robbers who, when pickings became thin, developed a taste for human flesh...

Arlene: maybe not just a tour guide for historical catastrophe but a latter day Pest Maiden, a millennial Typhoid Mary, rising from the depths of Boon's basement in a bloody butcher's apron, offering up her viral specials of the day. Plenty of contemporary killers to choose from, but maybe even one or two antique pathogens on special reserve. It wasn't entirely beyond the bounds of possibility that Arlene's nouvelle cuisine could have been tainted by some ancient bacterium, preserved in the very bricks used to seal up the doomed plague victims. If anthrax could survive seven hundred years, God knows what else might be lurking in history's middens.

Arlene: wining and dining her author on the unbleached calico chairs of Boon's, a single candle on the table. A late, intimate supper for two, Frankie boy might just have bitten off more than he could chew. ❑

A Hideous Jig

He is in Boon's, he knows it is Boon's but candles drip on raw wood trestles and blackened greasy walls drip with condensation. In the middle of the room, a fire spits; at its hearth, a pair of lean dogs snap and grizzle over a large bone. The dirt floor is littered with peelings, fruit pips, fish heads, scraps of gristle, dog shit.

Flies fizz and blister a steaming turd. A colony of rats noses through the pickings, nonchalant, proprietorial. Boon's but no art nouveau, no nouvelle cuisine for the nouveau riche; a beggar's banquet. At the table the toothless, shoeless and possibly mindless eat, drink and are more than merry; hysterical in fact, swilling down blue black wine and ramming food down their gullets, as if each mouthful were their last. On a nearby bench, a plump young woman and a vigorous young man gorge on each other. Seeing them so engrossed, a fat man in a gaping shirt, cheeks red as tomatoes, tongue wetly circling his mouth, plucks a turkey leg from the table and shoves it down the young woman's cleavage.

The woman squints at her breasts, pale and quivering like twin scoops of junket. The turkey leg glistens with grease. Her chin sinks into the folds of her neck. Her mouth drops open, tongue curls greedily towards the rounded tips of grey-pink bone. She pushes aside her young man and spreads her legs. The diners leer and drool. A second turkey leg is shove roughly into the depths of her filthy petticoats. Panting – from lust or lack of breath – the tomato cheeked man, his free hand closing on his crotch, pumps the plump woman full of turkey meat. Her moans are a mixture of pleasure and pain.

In an unlit booth, a wasted woman begins to beat a sombre, ponderous rhythm on an empty beer keg. The dogs raise their narrow heads. The rats are oblivious. The diners sup from mugs of ale or slump into their plates A voice, a cold, steely voice cuts through the belches and guffaws, the moans of misery and desire. The diners stagger to their feet and form a ramshacle chain. As one touches another, their rags crumble to the ground like long dead skin, revealing flesh riddled with dark blotches and swellings. A dry, rasping laughter crackles round the cavernous room as the procession lurches into a slow, hideous jig. Tongues balloon from mouths, lewd and stupid. The revelry swells but still doesn't drown out the ponderous beat of the drum nor the icy plainsong of the Pest Maiden, a tall, gaunt, hollow-eyed bag of bones, her distended shadow slithering across the floor. Here I have always been waiting in the dark. My time has come again.

The fires hisses, gasps. The room is hot as a furnace. The

procession stops at the bench. The leader stretches out his cankered hand. The fat man falls to his knees, the displaced lover covers his eyes and the plump woman throws back her head and screams....

Arlene is standing at the door of the kitchen. Her apron is bloody as a butcher's. With a sweep of her arm, she clears the table.

—So what have you decided on then? Listeria, salmonella, Ecoli, CJD. Or would you prefer something more traditional? ❏

CONTRIBUTORS

Simon Crump Born 1960 in Loughborough. Lived in Sheffield twenty years. *My Elvis Blackout*, a collection of short stories, is out with Clocktower Press, November 1998.

Des Dillon's most recent novel, *Duck* has been filmed as a BBC Scotland *Tartan Short*. His new novel *Itchycoo Blue* is issued in Spring 1999.

Lucy Ellman is currently a broad.

Eddie Gibbons is the author of no previous novels, being unable to tell his parse from his elbow. He lived in Liverpool between the Chatterley ban and the Beatles first LP. Consequently, he often uses the same words as Philip Larkin, but in a different order. He is writer in residence at the Inversnecky Snack Bar, Aberdeen.

Brian McCabe was born in Easthouses near Edinburgh, has lived as a writer since 1980. He has published two collections of poetry, two collections of short stories and a novel. *Low Life* is from his next collection of poems *Body Parts*, Canongate April 1999.

Duncan Mackay is the mystery man of this issue. His biog was lost in the post. Believed to hail from Lanarkshire.

Todd McEwen's ignorance knows no bounds, which is why he wanders in libraries and attaches himself to professors. He once shook Ian White's hand.

B. MacKenzie Gardiner Small Glaswegian person born in the year Everest was conquered. Loaned her concertina to a well known Edinburgh musician who claims it was subsequently stolen. If he reads this she's still waiting for her £100.

Ian Macpherson is an award-winning comedian. He has written plays and television scripts and a novel, which is to be published in 1999. He still lives in penury, a suburb of Sheffield.

Owen O'Neill is a comedy writer, poet stand-up comedian and film star. Amongst others, he starred in the film *Michael Collins* and is currently making people laugh in Los Angeles where they need this very badly.

Ian Rankin won the Crime Writers Association Gold Dagger Award for his novel Black & Blue, one of a critically acclaimed series featuring his popular Edinburgh-based detective Inspector Rebus.

Dylis Rose was born and brought up in Glasgow, now lives in Edinburgh and likes both cities. A play for stage, *Learning the Paso Doble* and *Pest Maiden*, a novel, are sue to appear in 1999.

R Eric Swanepoel was born in Edinburgh but brought up in southern Africa. Although a vet and a scientist he is wasting half his time in Paris writing a "humorous novel with political undertones" (left-wing, you may assume). His nose is currently buried in *Reading Jazz*, compiled by Robert Gottlieb, "the best book he has ever read", just like the last one.

David Tomassini Born and raised in East Lothian, he has lived in Italy for many years. Deliberately indecisive, he still alternates between white wine and red.